WHERE DO WE

GO WHEN WE

DIE?

BY

LORI BOYTERS

THIS BOOK

IS DEDICATED

TO ALL THOSE WHO SEEK THE TRUTH.

MAY THE LORD HELP YOU FIND TRUTH

THROUGH

HIS WORD

AND THAT

AMAZING

PEACE THAT

NO ONE

ELSE OR

NOTHING

ELSE CAN

GIVE.

This book is also dedicated to my dear friend and Bible teacher, Peter Barnes, 1928-2012. May he rest in peace knowing that his passion for teaching God's Word continues through his beloved students who were privileged to know him and learn the depths of God's Word from him. Please honor him by passing this on to someone else who needs to know the Truth.

What happens to us
when we die?

This has *always* been a major question that quietly nags at one's conscience and innermost being. Whether a person will admit it or not, deep in the recesses of their mind and spirit, that question remains *until* it is *completely satisfied*.

When a beloved friend or loved one dies, where do they *really* go? Years after they're gone, a fond memory of them triggers that nagging question again. Where are they right now? What are they doing? Do they really *still exist* somewhere? If so, where?

What do you believe?

Everyone *chooses* to believe *something* about what they *think* happens to them when they die. Some believe that because they're mostly a good person, they'll get into heaven somehow, or they think, "I'm not that bad. I try to do the right thing, which is more than most people." Some believe that they get another chance to live this life again (which is what I used to believe), and many believe that there is *just* nothingness. People have *chosen* to believe *something* to satisfy their soul, even if what they believe is dead wrong!

So, what if they're wrong? What's the big deal? They figure they're gonna find it out when they die anyway, so what's the hurry? BUT, *what if* waiting until they die to find out is *too late?*

> ## Even the choice to *believe in nothing,* is believing in *something.*

When I think about *trying* to believe in *nothing,* it takes a lot *more* faith than to believe in the *Truth,* which is the only thing we *must* believe in or the consequences *are* devastating, as I will explain later. There really is only *one* answer that satisfies, because there is really *only* one answer that is the truth.

I *know* without a shadow of a doubt the answer to this question. Not only do I know the answer to *this* question, but I also know the answer to the *other* question that is equally as nagging: *Why am I here?* We'll discuss this later, but for now, let's focus on the first question, *Where do we go when we die?*

The answer is very simple, yet most don't want to hear it and *certainly* don't want to believe it. Why not believe the only *real* Truth that satisfies the soul? So, where <u>do</u> we go when we die?

Answer: The Bible clearly says that Believers go to Heaven and non-believers go to Hades (or hell).

The Bible? "Oh brother," you might say, "that's so old fashioned." Or, "Only weak people still believe in that." With today's science and technology, you may even be thinking, "How can an intelligent, educated person still believe in that nonsense?"

I was a software test engineer for sixteen years for a major engineering firm. Although I'm not a genius by any means, I am educated and I know that what I know is the absolute truth, because as a test engineer, I've tested God's Word over and over and the results *always equal the Truth* – and that's the definition of *true* science.

Actually, some of the most intelligent and influential people who ever lived believed in the Holy Scriptures as the <u>only</u> Truth, such as:

Benjamin Franklin, George Washington, Abraham Lincoln, and many other brilliant and notable people.

History speaks of Albert Einstein as one of the most notable geniuses who ever lived. But, did you know that Sir Isaac Newton was a strong Believer in the Scriptures, and was a well-known scientist with an estimated IQ of 190![1] There are and have been many scientists and mathematicians[2] who believed in God and the Holy Scriptures. Most of our founding fathers of the United States of America were strong Believers, but you certainly didn't learn *that* in public school today – at least I know I didn't.

Do I have your attention yet? Please read on.

If only to merely satisfy your own curiosity, I encourage you to read on as I share with you how I found the answer many years ago. Knowing this has given me a final understanding of so many things about life *and death* that has brought a sense of peace to my soul. Isn't that what everyone *really* wants? Peace of mind?

---

[1] https://www.historytools.org/people/issac-newtons-iq
[2] https://www.famousscientists.org/great-scientists-christians/

Everyone *yearns* for peace of mind to fill that emptiness inside themselves that they can't quite put their finger on.

Is *this* really all there is? Many attempt to fill that emptiness with something (an education, a career, a loved one, family, sports, a hobby, or even *religion*), but there is only *One* answer that satisfies, and it is *none* of these things. And, it is especially *not religion*. These things only provide temporary satisfaction, but the emptiness *never* really goes away. Jesus said in John 8:32 "You will know the truth, and the truth will make you free."

What is your answer based on?

My answer is based on what's written in the Holy Scriptures (The Bible). God has given us *free will* to reject its truths; <u>but</u> that does *not* make it untrue. Many scholars, scientists, and non-believers have attempted to disprove it (to satisfy their own convictions), but *all have failed.* Of course, not all will admit it. To read overwhelming evidence that the Bible is the Truth, I recommend Josh McDowell's book *Evidence that Demands a Verdict.* Josh McDowell set out to disprove the Bible and discovered the overwhelming Truth of the Bible and became a Christian. One example from his book explains that there are over 300 major prophesies in the Old Testament that speaks of the coming Messiah. Jesus fulfilled each one of these. The mathematical odds of a human being fulfilling only 8 of these prophesies is about 1 in 10^{17}, which is about 1 in 100,000,000,000,000,000! Yet, Jesus fulfilled *all* of them! For more info on this, see http://www.jesus-is-lord.com/messiah.htm

Need more evidence?

Some people just got to have more evidence to prove God's existence. I can understand this today, because I grew up during a time in America where most folks believed in God without evidence. In the 1950's, in elementary school, we were encouraged to bow our heads and pray as someone said a short prayer over the load speaker. Yes, in public school. This stopped when an atheist, Madalyn Murray O'Hair, took her case to the Supreme Court to take prayer out of public school, which was approved by the court in 1962. Over the last sixty years, our culture has gone from this to actually teaching children that we evolved from apes or that we evolved from the Big Bang, with no actual scientific proof. Although there are no facts to support this theory, it is taught as if it *were* fact.

During my lifetime, I've seen our culture go from a society where people were ladies and gentlemen, children said yes sir and yes ma'am, people were polite and decent even if they weren't Christians, and even if they didn't agree with one another about politics, to what it is today. Today our society is all about taking God out of everything, especially our schools and universities, which has resulted in a society that is more selfish, greedy, hateful, noncaring, and corrupt, even at every level of government. Christians today are viewed as ignorant to believe in such nonsense that we all came from Adam and Eve. But, I do, and I never needed to be convinced. But today people need more evidence to wake them up to the Truth that they've been denied most of their life.

OK, here are a few gems of evidence I'll share with you if this helps. If these gems aren't enough to convince you of God's existence, His divine love and plan for mankind, and that there is no other way to Heaven, except through His son, Jesus, then you may as well stop reading this book and go about living your life the way you always have. But, also understand that at the end of your life, this question will come back and haunt you, "Where do we go when we die?" But then, it may be too late, but one thing is for sure, you WILL find out. One thing that we all have in common is that this life will end someday.

Let me ask you another question. Believing as you currently do, how's that working out for you? The Bible promises that when you become a true Believer, the Lord sends His Holy Spirit to indwell inside you and the resulting evidence of that is that you have this wonderful peace, and you have love, joy, patience, kindness, goodness, faithfulness, gentleness, and self-control (Galatians 5:22-23).

Do you have that peace that surpasses all understanding that God promises us in Philippians 4:7? Do you have love for others, even those who hurt you? Do you consider yourself a good and kind person? Have you ever stolen something or lied? What about self-control? Are you good at handling adversity? All these things God promises for His children. Why wouldn't a person want these things? Is pride keeping you from believing in God? In most cases, I do believe that is the main reason. People don't want to believe that they have been lied to, deceived, and even brainwashed by the enemy all their life. The Bible also says in Ephesians 6:12 that our true enemy is not people, but Satan and his fallen angels and demons. They are lying spirits and Satan is the author or father of lies (John 8:44) and deceit. Satan and his army have two jobs that they are extremely good at: 1) Keeping people from knowing the Truth, and 2) After they find the Truth, do everything they can to keep them from telling others by making them look like hypocrites so that others won't listen to them. If you want to find out more, please read on... So, here are a few gems of evidence that proves God's existence and that He truly is our creator.

We know God exists through creation and our conscience

The Apostle Paul wrote a letter to the new Believers in Rome, who were mostly Gentiles, to help them understand that mankind has no excuse for not believing in God as He has provided ample proof through creation and through our conscience.

Romans 1:18-27:

[18] *For the wrath of God is revealed from heaven against all ungodliness and unrighteousness of men, who by their unrighteousness suppress the truth.* [19] *For what can be known about God is plain to them, because God has shown it to them.* [20] *For His invisible attributes, namely, his eternal power and divine nature, have been clearly perceived, ever since the creation of the world, in the things that have been made. So, they are without excuse.* [21] *For although they knew God, they did not honor him as God or give thanks to him, but they became futile in their thinking, and their foolish hearts were darkened.* [22] *Claiming to be wise, they became fools,* [23] *and exchanged the glory of the immortal God for images resembling mortal man and birds and animals and creeping things.*
[24] *Therefore God gave them up in the lusts of their hearts to impurity, to the dishonoring of their bodies among themselves,* [25] *because they exchanged the truth about God for a lie and worshiped and served the creature rather than the Creator, who is blessed forever! Amen.*
[26] *For this reason God gave them up to dishonorable passions. For their women exchanged natural relations for those that are contrary to nature;* [27] *and the men likewise gave up natural relations with women and were consumed with passion for one another, men committing shameless acts with men and receiving in themselves the due penalty for their error.*

There is much evidence in nature of intelligent design (a Creator). For example, ever heard of the Bombardier Beetle? It could have never evolved because of the design of its safety defense mechanism as I will explain. The

Bombardier Beetle is a little ground beetle less than an inch in size, which is found in North and South America, Europe, Africa, and Australia. https://www.nwf.org/Educational-Resources/Wildlife-Guide/Invertebrates/Bombardier-Beetles

What makes this little beetle unique is that it has two small chambers in its abdomen that hold two reactant chemicals. When disturbed, the beetle squeezes out a small amount of these chemicals and when they combine, they create a chemical reaction that brings the temperature up to water's boiling point. While the one-way valve closes to protect the beetle's organs, out fires the mixture of gas and steam at 212 degrees Fahrenheit (100°C). The beetle then has perfect aim to fire the chemical at its predator. How could this little beetle have evolved to this point without blowing itself up?

Here's another example. Did you know that our Earth is able to sustain life because it is the perfect distance from the Sun? Any closer and we'd burn up, any further and we'd freeze to death. There are many factors in nature which must exist at the same time to support life on Earth.

Did you know that recent studies in DNA prove that an intelligent designer had to have created this amazing genetic code that defines each one of us uniquely? http://magazine.biola.edu/article/10-summer/can-dna-prove-the-existence-of-an-intelligent-desi/

Did you know that recent archeological finds prove the Bible?
https://biblearchaeology.org/

Through our conscience

Does an animal have a guilty conscience after they've killed and eaten their prey? Of course not. Does a human have a guilty conscience if they steal something that doesn't belong to them? Of course. This is what distinguishes humans from animals. God gave us a conscience to ensure order by knowing what is right and what is wrong. The primary reason God had to destroy life on earth with a flood was because the world and mankind had become so corrupt that if He hadn't done this, mankind would have been completely wiped out.

The conscience is a supernatural feature, like our spirit and soul, that God designed within us to be like Him, so that He could interface with us. In Genesis 1:26, it says "We will make them in Our likeness." Who is We and Our? Father, Son (Jesus), and the Holy Spirit.

The ONLY Truth is God's Word (The Bible)

With so many advances in technology and science today, the Bible still remains the best seller of *all* books ever written. Imagine that! *All books ever written!* In fact, according to Wikipedia (http://en.wikipedia.org/wiki/List_of_best-selling_books), no other books even come close to the Bible in sales. The Bible leads the list with between 2.5 to 6 billion copies sold to date. The next highest best-seller is *The Little Red Book-Quotations from Chairman Mao.* However, this was because the Chinese communist government paid between $600 to $6.5 billion to have copies printed, of which only about a third were purchased, with the rest placed in stock or in stores. The Chinese dictator, Mao Zedong, between 1964 and 1976 forced everyone to carry one with them at all times.

The more I study the Bible, the more I learn about God and why I'm here, what my purpose is, and where I'm going. I challenge you to test it out for yourself. Open it and read it. Its Words are powerful, are everlasting, and they penetrate the soul, because it is *truly* the living, breathing Word of God. To coin a quote from an old-southern farmer, as far as I'm concerned, "IF GOD SAID IT! I BELIEVE IT! AND THAT SETTLES IT!"

Who wrote the Bible?

The Bible was written by men but inspired by God as to what they should write. 2 Timothy 3:16 states that, "All scripture is inspired by God and profitable for teaching, for reproof, for correction, for training in righteousness, so that the man (i.e., mankind – men, women, and children) of God may be adequate, equipped for every good work." The Bible is God's letter to humanity to help us to know who He is, why we are here, how He wants us to live, and where we are going after this earthly life. Have men changed God's Word over time, especially with the many translations? Yes, but His overall message has not changed. That He loves us so much, He sent His son to die for us so that we could be saved from the punishment of our sins. 1 John 4:14.

> ## The Bible was written by men, but *inspired by God Himself.*

It was written over the course of 1500 years by forty men of vastly different backgrounds, from world rulers and fishermen.

In a sense, I can understand how God can inspire people to write down what He wants people to know because of my experience with writing this little book. When the idea came to me to write this (thinking at first it was my own), it was out of my deep concern for my dear precious unsaved family members and friends.

So, this information started out to be just for them, but then I began to think (or at least I thought it was me) of so many others who could benefit from reading this book too. Next thing I knew, ideas were flooding into my mind about what things I should write. I can only attribute that inspiration to *God's Holy Spirit* within me, which I'll cover in more detail later.

Now let's get back to the question, *Where do we go when we die?*

Only Believers go to Heaven when they die.

A Believer goes straight to heaven (where God is) (Luke 23:43, John 14:2-4, Acts 7:55-56, 2 Corinthians 12:4, Revelation 2:7). *No one* can go to heaven unless they are a Believer. Jesus said in John 14:6, "I am the way, and the truth, and the life; *no one* comes to the Father, *but* through Me." The Bible also says that "There is a way which *seems right* to man, but its end is the way of death (separation from God)." Proverbs 16:25.

You are either a Believer or a non-believer. That's the only way God sees it.

A Believer is a true Christian. I say *true Christian* because there are many who say they are a Christian, but are not and they are only fooling themselves. A *true* Christian or Believer is one who has the Holy Spirit indwelling within them, Who guides them into all Truth. A true Believer follows Jesus Christ our Lord and Savior and *believes in their heart* that Jesus is God and that God loves them so much (John 3:16) that He came in a human body (Jesus is God incarnate, Matthew 2:23, John 10:30, John 14:7, Mikah 5) around 2000 years ago for the purpose of dying on the cross (to become the final sacrifice) to wash away all our sins (Romans 5:8). And – most important – that He rose from the grave and conquered death – and is now alive sitting at the right hand of God reigning in heaven (Hebrews 12:2) and has given us His Holy Spirit to reside within us forever (Acts 2:4, Acts 11:15, Romans 8:9). The Believer does not _merely_ just *believe* this, because the Bible says that even Satan and the demons believe in God and Jesus, *and shudder* (James 2:19). We also *must* have an *active* faith, which is the evidence that we are a true Believer. If you are a *true* Believer, you will feel bad about your sin, repent, and want to tell others about how He changed your life for the better. James, the brother of Jesus, said "Faith without works is useless (or dead)" (James 2:20). What does this mean? If you truly have faith in something, you will not only *tell* others about it, but will do your best to *convince* them that it's true.

Everything has been done that needs to be done for you to be saved. Jesus died on the cross once for all times for everyone. Jesus said *"It is finished!"* (John 19:30). The greatest words ever uttered by the greatest Man who ever lived! Jesus Christ. All you need to do is accept it and *believe it!*

Christianity is NOT a religion, it's a relationship.

To become a Believer, who is forever forgiven from all your sins (past, present, *and future*), all you need to do is put your *faith and trust* in the Lord Jesus Christ and *believe with all your heart* that what He did for you on the cross was real. **God made it simple on purpose!** We cannot save ourselves from the punishment of our sins, and God says that we are *all* sinners (Romans 3:23) and there has to be a sacrifice to wash away the punishment for our sin – Jesus did that on the cross, once and for all. "The Father has sent the Son to be the Savior of the world." (1 John 4:14).

Once we become a Believer, we are included into God's family and our relationship with Him begins.

There is only ONE way to get to heaven.

One truth that mankind has a hard time accepting, because they believe it to be narrow minded, is that there is *only* one way to heaven, through Jesus Christ. I didn't say this, Jesus said this in John 14:6 "I am the way, and the truth, and the life; no one comes to the Father but through Me." And again Proverbs 14:12 says "There is a way which seems right to man, but the end is the way of death (or separation from God)." If you are not a Believer, you are a non-believer. God sees mankind as either *one* or the *other*.

But you say it's too hard to change.

This is *very* true. Even the Apostle Paul struggled with this even up until he died (Romans 7:15-20). You cannot change yourself on the inside, only God can do that. This is *why* we need a Savior. When we make that commitment to trust Jesus as our Lord and Savior, the Bible says that His Holy Spirit comes to reside permanently inside us (1 Corinthians 3:16, 6:19) and creates in us a new and clean heart and attitude (Ephesians 4:17-24). We are actually changed from the inside and become like a new creature in Christ (2 Corinthians 5:17). It's like our very core is changed.

If we are truly one of His, the Holy Spirit inside us is very subtle and gently convicts us when we do something that offends God. If we desire in our heart to turn from that sin, God's

Holy Spirit gives us the power to overcome it (Ephesians 6:10, Philippians 4:13, and James 4:7-8). If you are living in habitual sin and don't have any really strong convictions about it, you may *not* be a true Believer, because believe me, God will not allow you to ignore it for very long.

God continually amazes me when I see His hand at work in my life. Especially when He sets me free from negative things I've struggled with for so many years. I'm left with no desire to return to them. In fact, it makes me sick to my stomach to even think about ever doing it again, like when I used to smoke – yuk! Some things take longer than others, but if we have the faith to endure, He WILL help us to overcome it and replace that former drive (the Bible calls it our fleshly desire) with a peace that surpasses all understanding (Philippians 4:7, Galatians 5:16) and rewards us for hanging in there until the end (1 Corinthians 3:12-15, Rev. 22:12).

John 3:30, "He must increase, but I must decrease." After we become a Believer, we will still sin. If we continue in our sin and have no desire to change, we cannot lose our salvation, but we can actually *grieve* the Holy Spirit (or stop the flow of what the Holy Spirit wants to accomplish through us) (Ephesians 4:30). As I just said, I believe that the Bible teaches that we <u>cannot</u> lose our salvation. If you don't believe me, read the Bible on this subject as it is very clear that we cannot: John 10:28 (Jesus gives us *eternal* life – *eternal* means *forever*), John 11:26, Romans 5:8-9, 2 Corinthians 5:21, Ephesians 1:13, Titus 3:5, Hebrews 13:5c. Jesus emphasizes this in John 10:28:26-29 when he told the Jews, "You do not believe, because you are not of My sheep. My sheep hear My voice, and I know them, and they follow Me; and I give them eternal life, and they shall *never* perish; and no one can snatch them out of My hand. My Father, who has given them to Me, is greater than all; and no one is able to snatch them out of the Father's hand." This includes YOU. I'm so thankful for this promise, so I don't have to worry that I can do anything to lose my salvation. If you are in a church that teaches otherwise; run away from that church as fast as you can and find one that teaches the Truth.

Our willingness to continue in our sin can slow down or even stop our spiritual growth to where we feel stagnant until we deal with our sin.

Even after over 40 years since I accepted Christ as my Savior on June 12th, 1981, I am still learning and growing in my faith. The Lord has helped me get free from cigarettes, cussing, a *bad* temper, anger, bitterness, and so many other things. Although I'm still working on the quick temper problem, He is always prompting me through His Holy Spirit to continually renew my mind, which improves my attitude and gives me even more peace, patience, and self-control. I will *never* reach perfection while I am in this human body; neither will any of us. If you have turned away from God because of something *someone who calls themselves a Christian* did, please, please don't blame God for that. Christians are targets by Satan and his minions. As soon as you become a Christian, you *will* become a target. But, if you stay close to the Lord, He promises to protect you. James 4:7-8 says, "Resist the devil and he will flee from you. Draw near to God and He will draw near to you". How do you draw near to God? Pastor Miles McPherson used to say that we should be PRO Christians (PRO = Pray, Read, Obey). When things begin to go wrong in your life, ask yourself if you are doing these things, if not, *get started* and it's amazing to see how fast things change for the better.

Satan wants to make you look bad by exposing your sins to others because he knows that exposing your sin to non-believers makes you look like a hypocrite, which makes God look bad, then this can cause people to turn away from God. This is why God tells us in His Word that we should put on His spiritual armor to protect us from the evil one (Ephesians 6:10-17). If *you* don't want to look like a hypocrite and turn others away from God, do your best to study His Word and turn from the negative things that you brought into your life. Trust Him and He will deliver you from these things. I have seen tons of folks delivered from alcohol, drugs, pornography, smoking, cursing, anger, bad tempers, bad attitudes, jealousy, food addictions, idolatry, cheating, lying – you name it! He will free you from these things – you just need to ask Him and then *believe* (have faith) that He will.

Not long ago, I was beginning to be convicted of something that I was doing that I hadn't really thought of as sin. I especially didn't think of it as something interfering with my relationship with God. I was slowly beginning to understand as my spirit was made aware of this by the subtle prompting of the Holy Spirit within me. It may sound silly to you, but it wasn't silly to God.

I had been watching a soap opera every week faithfully for over eight years. When I first started watching it, it wasn't that bad, but, as the years went on, it slowly introduced more acts of immorality. I became drawn in by the characters almost like I knew them, so I easily overlooked or compromised on many otherwise blatant indiscretions. I found myself fascinated by their continual drama and stayed tuned in each week to find out how they were going to get out of this one? Their drama and indiscretions included sexual immorality, divorce, cheating, lying, etc, which were all things that displeased God. That's one of Satan's primary means of deception – to cause us to become addicted to our sins. It begins innocently enough, then over time, it subtlety gets worse until you are "hooked". Because I knew it wasn't *real*, "These people are only actors," I'd rationalize. So, I'd justify to myself that it was ok to watch. But the closer I got to God, the more He revealed things to me in my life that I needed to "clean up" because they were dishonoring to Him. Believe me, I still have more stuff to "clean up", as we all do. The Lord will never be finished with us in this area.

Now if someone had told me "You shouldn't be watching that stuff, it offends God! And, you call yourself a Christian?" I know that I would have defended myself to the core! But because the Holy Spirit convicted me from within, I had no choice but to listen and obey out of my love and respect for Him. THAT is how *real* change happens in a Christian's life. This is what makes Christianity different from religions, God changes your heart. Would God still love me if I didn't give up watching the soap opera? Of course. But, because I love Him and appreciate all that He's done for me, I didn't want to offend Him, so I stopped watching it. Now here it is years later, and I don't even miss it. In fact, I have more time now to do other things that are more productive.

After I made that decision to stop watching the soap opera, I did notice that a host of good things suddenly came my way. I received a large bonus from work, and our non-profit organization received a huge donation from the company I work for. Not that God's grace always works this way. Sometimes we receive an extra measure of grace out of the blue when we haven't done anything to deserve it. That's why it's called grace. Grace is a free gift from God that we don't deserve. This is because God loves us so much. Pay attention next time this happens to you and don't forget to thank the Lord for His amazing grace, mercy, and forgiveness. It was as though God wanted to bless me, but my watching the soap opera was *grieving the Holy Spirit;* thus, "preventing the flow" of what He wanted to do for me and *through* me. What a hypocrite I was watching this soap opera, yet teaching God's Word to children on Sunday morning, instructing them to *not* do the very things I was condoning by watching that soap opera. See how the enemy works? When the lie is exposed (brought into the light), Jesus will restore you with the Truth. The more you grow in your faith, the more aware you become of God's Holy Spirit in your life and what His will is for you.

Where is Heaven? Where is hell?

According to the Bible, heaven and hell are in a place that you can only reach *after* death. Most Bible scholars believe that the Biblical evidence points to the location of heaven as being outside the universe, and that the location of hell is in the center of the earth. Satan, the fallen angels, and demons will be thrown into the Lake of Fire (believed to be outside the universe) in the end and the non-believers that have been in hell since the beginning of mankind, will then be thrown into the Lake of Fire for eternity as well. There is no other place to go. You either go to heaven or hell. Hell is a place of continual torment (Mark 9:48, Luke 16:23). Some even laugh and say, "Oh well, if I'm going to hell, at least I'll be there with my friends." This is a lie! Many Bible scholars agree that in hell there is no contact with other humans. You are alone and separated from God for eternity, but you may still hear the continual screams of torment from others. What a horrible place!

> **God does not send people to hell – they *choose* to go there when they reject God.**

When people die today, as stated previously, the Bible says they either go to paradise (heaven) to be with Jesus or they go to hell to await the *Great White Throne Judgment* at the end of the world. (Revelation 20:11-15).

When is the end of the world?

No one knows when the end of the world will be (Matthew 24:4-31, Luke 21:8-28). Jesus said in Matthew 24:36, "But of that day and hour no one knows, not even the angels of heaven, nor the Son, but the Father alone." Did you read that right? NOT even Jesus knew! Some scholars say that this was only when Jesus was in human form because He was limited while inside a human body.

Many have predicted this and have failed and looked foolish. Beware of those who say they know when the end of time will be or when Jesus is returning - no one knows. But the Bible does talk of the "signs of the times" (Matthew 24) that will indicate we are getting close to the end of time as we know it. Some of those signs are already evident in the world today, such as world wars, a huge rise in moral decay and corruption, major famines and earthquakes in diverse places. Evil is becoming more and more wicked and prevalent. People don't try to hide it as much anymore. In fact, many sins that were mostly hidden in the past are now out in the open. Some are even proud of their sins, and many sins that were considered repulsive for most of humankind's existence, are now considered normal.

The main thing to look for to know that the end is coming soon is the rebuilding of the third Jewish temple in Jerusalem. Because the Antichrist cannot be revealed until the temple is built (Daniel 12:11, Matthew 24:15, Mark 13:14, Luke 21:20, and described in Rev. 17). The last seven years of life as we know it, before Jesus returns is called the Tribulation period. Although many theologians believe that the rapture will come at the beginning, middle, or end of this Tribulation period, most believe it will come before the Tribulation begins. There are verses that can support each view, but I basically hope it comes before, but if not, I trust that the Lord will protect me through it. Should I die now or during the Tribulation, it matters not to me, because I know where I'm going for eternity, and that gives me great comfort.

This is all explained in the Book of Revelation written by John, Jesus' disciple. It's a very difficult book to understand because John was taken up into heaven by God and shown how the world will end. Some of the things John saw were so amazing and bazaar that it was difficult to describe. But I'll try to summarize what I've learned from years of study on this book. I would like to give my dear, dear friend, Peter Barnes, most of the credit for what I've learned about this amazing book. He knew more about the Bible than any man I've ever known. He was *truly* a man of God and was gifted with an amazing understanding of God's Word and the ability to teach it to simple-minded people like myself.

As told in the Book of Revelation, the *Tribulation period* is believed to be a seven-year period (Rev 6:1 through Chapter 19) when the Antichrist (a man possessed by Satan himself) will control the world until Jesus comes with the Believers from heaven to earth to fight against the Antichrist and their human armies during the famous *Battle of Armageddon.* Jesus and the Believers win the war of course, and Satan is thrown into the Abyss (aka Bottomless Pit) for 1000 years, and Jesus rules on earth with the Believers.

You would think that if Satan and his minions were out of the picture, the world would be like a perfect place to live right? Not true! Remember, people continue to be born and they are *still* sinners from birth. People continue to have children and when they become adults, they will *still* choose to sin and *still* choose to reject God. I believe that God created this period to show mankind that they can't blame Satan any longer when they *choose* to sin.

Following the Millennium, Satan is released from the Abyss, and he gathers together a huge army of non-believers in an attempt to overthrow Jerusalem.

God will not allow them a chance to cause any harm to the Believers. God will send fire down from heaven to incinerate them in an instant (Revelation 20:9). Satan is then thrown into the Lake of Fire with his fallen angels and demons, and the non-believers are thrown into hell to await the *Great White Throne Judgment.*

Finally, all non-believers who ever lived that have been waiting in hell are released by God to appear before Him at the *Great White Throne Judgment*. Each person will be judged and will receive their sentence for eternity based on the sinful things they did when they were alive. Then God will throw them all into the Lake of Fire where they will reside for eternity in torment.

Non-believers will be judged once and for all!

God will create a brand-new glorious heaven and earth (Rev 21), and a new city of Jerusalem where all the Believers will reign forever with Jesus! Praise the Lord!!!

How do we know that all this is true?

Because this is what the Bible says, and the Bible is God's Word. For more convincing evidence on why I believe the Bible is true, take a look at:

www.christiananswers.net/q-eden/edn-t003.html.

I also recommend that you read *A Case for Christ* by Lee Strobel. Lee was a devout atheist and award-winning investigative journalist for the Chicago Tribune. He was determined to debunk Christianity when his wife became a Christian to convince her to turn away from what she believed, which he believed to be nonsense. To his surprise, through his excellent journalistic analysis and research, he discovered that the case for Christ's existence and His claim of being God was so overwhelming, that he became a Believer himself. He now teaches what he believes all over the world. https://leestrobel.com/about/

If you are honest with yourself, you *want* all this to be true, and you *want* to understand it and believe it too. But something is keeping you from believing this. I believe that much of it is human pride and deception. So, what do you have to lose if you don't believe it?

Do you get defensive or offended when you hear this stuff? You may even get angry when you hear someone speak to you about Jesus, especially Jesus Christ. Why is that? Do you get angry if someone talks about Buddha or Mohammad or even God? Probably not. But, when you hear the name *Jesus*, especially *Jesus Christ*, does that hit a cord deep inside you? The Bible says that there is *power* in that name (John 1:12). Remember, Satan hates and fears Him and is a master at finding ways to deceive you and keep you from knowing the truth about God.

So, what do you have to lose?

Your soul and spirit are the essence of who you really are. The soul and spirit do not die and exist forever, but *where* it resides is up to you. Why take this risk when there is so much to gain, but so very much to lose? If you reject Jesus Christ, the only heaven you will ever know, is this life on earth you are experiencing now.

Even if it turns out that there is nothingness or we get another chance at life, we Believers still have gained much in this life – love, joy, peace, patience, kindness, goodness, faithfulness, gentleness, self-control, (Galatians 5:22-23) and so much more – which is what all humans have strived for since the beginning of time. But, if the Bible is correct, and every fiber of my being knows that it is, those who don't take the opportunity to accept Christ as their Savior, will live in torment forever in hell. Do you really want to take that chance? Don't let pride prevent you from opening your heart to Him. The Bible says that pride comes before *the fall* (Proverbs 16:18).

The Bible says that Satan is the ruler of this world (2 Corinthians 4:4) – that God gave him that authority. God allows Satan to rule over the earth until he is thrown into the Lake of Fire in the end. Satan, the fallen angels, and demons have had thousands of years to figure out how to fool mankind into thinking: there is no God who cares, there is no heaven or hell, we get another chance after death, get everything you can out of life because we only live once, or that there are many ways to get to heaven. The Bible clearly says that Satan is the master deceiver and father of all lies. (Rev 12:9).

Satan knows how weak we humans are, which makes him angrier knowing that God loves us so much more than the angels because he died on the cross for us – not even for the angels. And, it makes Satan furious to know that according to the Bible, when humans go to heaven, they will even judge the angels! (1 Corinthians 6:3).

Satan knows the end of the story! He only has a specific amount of time left to deceive us and he wants to take as many of us with him as he can to the Lake of Fire, because he knows how much that will hurt God. What chance do we weak humans have against such a power as Satan, except when God gives us His power to protect us from him and his minions. (Romans 8:38 and Ephesians 6:10-17).

You do not know when your life will end. It could end any minute.

If you die right now, do you want to absolutely be sure of where you're going?

In Rev 3:20, Jesus says "Behold, I stand at the door and knock." He is knocking on your heart right now at this very moment whether you realize it or not. "If anyone hears My voice and opens the door (to your heart), I will come into him and will dine with him and he with Me." That is, His Holy Spirit will come inside you to live forever. If you keep resisting Him, He is a gentleman and will eventually stop trying. Heaven help you if that ever happens. The Bible says in 2 Peter 2:21 "For it would be better for them not to have known the way of righteousness, than having known it and turned away." And *now,* because you have read this information, you can't say you didn't know the Truth. I pray to the Lord that you stop resisting Him. You *never* know if *this* will be the last time He tries.

I was once asked by a non-believer, "So, after the Christians are raptured won't everyone remaining finally believe that what they were saying was true, and then they will finally believe and become Christians too?" The Bible says (2 Thessalonians 2:10-12) that those who rejected Christ prior to the rapture and remain will not have the opportunity to accept Him because God will send them a deluding spirit so that they will believe what is false. So, no, they won't be given another chance to accept Jesus if they had already rejected Him. How do you know if you've rejected Him you might ask? Well, when you finish reading this book, I don't see how you can stand before God and say you didn't know about what Jesus did for you on the cross, and what you needed to do to accept Him as your Savior.

How to be saved

Say this prayer out loud to God right now, and *mean it* with your heart, and you WILL be saved (Rom 10:9, 13). It's that simple! God made it simple on purpose.

"Lord Jesus, I need you. Thank you for dying on the cross for my sins. Thank you for your grace and for forgiving me of my sins. I confess and repent of my sins. Right this moment, I trust you as my Savior and Lord. I believe that you died on the cross for my sins and rose again from the dead three days later and are now sitting at the right hand of the Father. Please give me the power to overcome the sins in my life that offend you and help me to become the person you created me to be. In Jesus Christ's name. Amen."

If you just prayed this prayer and meant it in your heart, you are saved *forever* and God just sent His Holy Spirit to live inside of you – even if you didn't feel anything! Wow! Hallelujah! Although you may not have noticed right away that the Holy Spirit is now dwelling inside you, you will begin to notice it more and more as you grow in your faith. You will especially notice that the way you think about things will continue to change. Almost like the light finally went on! You will begin to have more peace, be less and less angry and impatient, care for others more, even those who hurt you, and so many more wonderful changes will happen in your heart, mind, and spirit. As you grow in your faith, you will experience more and more positive changes in your heart (this is called the sanctification process). To grow in your faith daily, pray (talk to God), trust God for everything, read and study His Word daily, obey Him in everything you do, say, and even think, because it is for your own good believe me. Fellowship with other Believers and share your faith with others so that they can know the Lord too and be with us in heaven forever with God.

Why would God make it so easy?

Because of His amazing grace and love for us. (Romans 10:9, 11:6, Ephesians 2:8-9, John 3:16). After all, the definition of love is…. God. (1 John 4:7-16).

So, why am I here?

Now that's the other *nagging* question. Are we here just to experience God's peace and forgiveness and be assured of our salvation (so that we are saved from our sins, so we get to go to heaven)? No. This is definitely the first requirement, but God has a plan for each of us, and not just for our life on earth, but for what we will ultimately be doing for eternity in heaven with Him, His angels, and other Believers. Once you've accepted Christ as your Savior, that is *only* the beginning of your new and amazing journey towards learning what God's plan is for you on this earth and beyond. But, ultimately as part of our journey on earth, His Holy Spirit will gently guide and direct you towards what He has called all Christians to do, which is to…

> **Love others, tell them about His sacrificial love for them, and even love those who persecute you.**

This is what pleases God more than ANYTHING! This is *active* faith.

Believe me I understand how hard it is to love my enemies. But this is what He requires us to do. Once you start praying for them, you will be amazed at what God can do. There is such amazing power in prayer. You cannot do this on your own, only God can give you the ability to love others who persecute you.

How will people be saved if someone doesn't tell them about God's Truth? (Romans 10:17). *This* is every Christians' purpose in life. If you let Him, God will use the talents He has given you to reach others with the Truth.

God gave me the gift of writing and teaching, so I enjoy using my gifts for Him to write this information for you and others to read. Some are given the gift of singing, some of playing music, some have a passion for teaching, and others enjoy helping others. Got it? All these gifts could be used to help others know about Jesus Christ. Unfortunately, too many use their God-given gifts for selfish reasons, which many times becomes their downfall - just look at people in the movie industry, politics, and sports – so many lives are destroyed because they sell themselves out for fame and fortune. But, it's never too late to turn that around. As long as there is breath in your body, there is still hope for change. What gift or gifts did God give to you? I tell you the truth, that when you use your gift to help others know the Lord, it is the most exhilarating and fulfilling experience you'll ever know. This is because *this* is what God *designed* us to do – it's our primary objective while we are alive in our physical bodies here on earth.

Before I became a Christian, I had a passion for surfing and loved to compete. Surfing a huge wave and "pulling it off" was the most exhilarating experience I've ever had before I accepted Christ as my Savior.

So, what do you do now?

If you put your faith and trust in Him, He will direct your paths, and you will be blessed with peace through all circumstances. God promises his children (all Believers) that "all things work together for good to those who love God, to those who are called according to His purpose." (Romans 8:28) This does not mean that you will never have troubles again, it means that *when* troubles come – and they will, He is there to protect you and help you through it.

Read your Bible and learn about His Truths so that you can tell others. Find a good Bible-believing church or small study group and start attending weekly to learn more about God and Jesus and your new faith. There are many churches that profess to teach the Bible as God's truth, but be careful, as there are many false prophets out there too. Trust God to lead you to the right church. We are blessed to live in a country where there are many good churches, but I recommend the Calvary Chapel churches, the Christian and Missionary Alliance churches, and the Baptist churches to name a few, as I have personally attended these over the years and although I may not agree with them 100% of the time, most of what they teach I agree with. I recommend reading a Bible that was published by Thomas Nelson Publishers, Zondervan, or Tyndale House Publishers, as I believe that you can trust these versions. I recommend the "Life Application Study Bible" published by Tyndale House Publishers for new Believers, because it is easy to read. As for me, I actually enjoy using the "New American Standard Version (NASV), published by Thomas Nelson Publishers, because I've learned that it is the closest English version that reflects the original meaning from the original languages (Hebrew-Old Testament; Greek and Aramaic-New Testament), but it is written more at a college level, so it's a little harder read. Another good one is the *John MacArthur Study Bible.* John provides commentary on every single verse in the Bible!

If you're too shy to tell others about Him – just give them this little book, pray for them, and God will do the rest.

God has been waiting for you and will start you on this most amazing and wonderful journey with Him as soon as you agree to accept Him as your Savior and Lord!

If you have questions or comments about what I've written here or any other Bible questions, please send them to wheredowegowhenwedie@gmail.com and I'll do my best to provide you with the correct answer as it relates to Scripture.

I'm just a regular person who loves God and wants others to know Him too. Although I'm not a Bible scholar with fancy degrees, I've studied and taught children God's Word for over 30 years under some amazingly Godly teachers, pastors, and Bible scholars, along with the guidance of the Holy Spirit as I continue to read and study His most excellent Word. The Lord will gladly teach you too if you will only open it and read it for yourself and trust Him to guide you.
My prayer for you is:

"Lord, please protect the person reading this little book and give them a desire in their heart to want to continually seek after You and Your Truth and come to know You as their personal Lord and Savior. In Jesus' name. Amen."

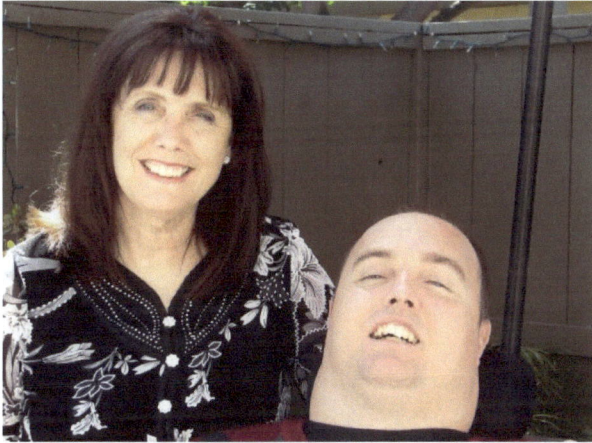

Lori Boyters and her quadriplegic son, Bobby DuCharme, are the co-founders of *Can't Keep Me Down*, a non-profit organization that helps paralyzed victims and their families with the difficult transition of dealing with life as a paraplegic or quadriplegic. Their organization also develops inspirational films and literature to help others find peace with the Lord through their tragic circumstances.

Bobby broke his neck surfing on June 1st, 1999 and has created and published many surfing films since his accident. He enjoys sharing his faith through his films.

To find out more about them and their organization, visit:

www.cantkeepmedown.org.

I made a video of this book a while back if you would like to check it out and share it with others you care about.
God Bless,

Lori and Bobby

Video Book at:
https://www.youtube.com/watch?v=ye5CPt94xC0&t=2s